HAUNTED HISTORY

PHANTOM SOLDIERS
and Other Gettysburg Hauntings

by Megan Cooley Peterson

CAPSTONE PRESS
a capstone imprint

Capstone Captivate is published by Capstone Press, an imprint of Capstone.
1710 Roe Crest Drive
North Mankato, Minnesota 56003
www.capstonepub.com

Library of Congress Cataloging-in-Publication Data is available on the Library of Congress website.
ISBN: 978-1-4966-8369-4 (library binding)
ISBN: 978-1-4966-8420-2 (eBook PDF)

Summary: Phantom cries from wounded soldiers echo through the air. Strange orbs of light appear in photographs. These stories and more are found at Gettysburg Battlefield, the site of a historical American Civil War battle. Readers will follow along in spooky delight as they discover the ghosts of Gettysburg, Pennsylvania.

Image Credits
Alamy: Chesh, middle 15, History and Art Collection, left 29, JG Photography, top 21, Jon Bilous, 16; Newscom: AIWire, 9, MARK MAKELA/REUTERS, 27, Remsberg Inc, 19, World History Archive, 7; Pixabay: dannysantos, (wood) design element, geralt, (paper) design element; Shutterstock: Allison Stec Bell, 17, Arie v.d. Wolde, 10, Askolds Berovskis, Cover, Christian Hinkle, Cover, ComicSans, (smoke) Cover, DeZet, 24, Everett Historical, 11, bottom right 15, Linda Bucklin, Cover, Mama Belle and the kids, 18, Motortion Films, 26, Timothy Robert Weikert, 5, George Sheldon, 23, woodsnorthphoto, middle right 21; Wikimedia: Armistead46, 13, Library of Congress/Charles J. Tyson, 25, Smallbones, bottom right 29

Editorial Credits
Editor: Renae Gilles; Designer: Sara Radka; Media Researcher: Morgan Walters; Production Specialist: Spencer Rosio

All internet sites appearing in back matter were available and accurate when this book was sent to press.

Printed and bound in the USA.
PA117

TABLE OF CONTENTS

Words in **bold** are in the glossary.

A NEVER-ENDING BATTLE?

In July 1863, the Battle of Gettysburg waged for three days. The United States was in the middle of the Civil War (1861–1865). The Union wanted to keep the nation together. The Confederates wanted to break away from the United States. Each side fought to the death for its cause.

Many people believe the **ghosts** of some who died never left. Gettysburg, Pennsylvania, may be one of America's most haunted places. The city was first settled in the late 1700s. By the time of the battle, it had grown to almost 2,500 citizens. Its battlefields aren't the only spots said to be visited by ghosts. Many other places around the city are reportedly haunted too.

FREAKY FACT

More than 150,000 soldiers fought at the Battle of Gettysburg.

Gettysburg Battlefield is known as one of the most haunted battlefields in the United States.

THE ANGLE

TIMELINE OF THE BATTLE OF GETTYSBURG

June 30, 1863—Confederates spot Union soldiers near Gettysburg.

July 1, 1863—The fighting begins at McPherson's Ridge in Gettysburg.

July 2, 1863—Union soldiers defend Little Round Top.

July 3, 1863—The Confederates retreat. The Union army wins.

CHAPTER 1

THE BATTLEFIELDS

Today, the old battlefields of Gettysburg are a peaceful national park. But in July 1863, blood and screams filled the valley. Many men died there. The battlefields have been ghostly hot spots for more than 150 years.

DEVIL'S DEN

On July 2, Union and Confederate soldiers fought at Devil's Den. Soldiers took cover behind large rocks and boulders. But the rocky ground meant soldiers couldn't dig **trenches**.

Many men on both sides died during the fighting at Devil's Den. The Confederates drove out the Union. But the ghosts of dead soldiers may have stuck around.

More than 50,000 soldiers were injured or killed on the Gettysburg battlefields.

Many people say Devil's Den is one of Gettysburg's most haunted places. Cameras, phones, and watches stop working when visitors reach the rocks. Many people have reported seeing a ghostly soldier. He walks among the rocks. The man wears a floppy hat and ragged clothing. He has long hair. A Texas **regiment** was heavily involved in the Confederate victory. Members dressed in a similar style to what the ghost is seen wearing.

One of the first sightings was in the 1970s. A woman was walking through the maze of rocks with her camera. She was about to snap a photo. Then she felt something—or someone—next to her. A man with a floppy hat and torn clothing stood at her side. The man pointed and said, "What you're looking for is over there." The woman looked in the direction the man pointed to. When she looked back at the man, he had disappeared. Since then, others have reported the same haunting experience. Have they all seen the same ghost?

The rocky terrain at Devil's Den made fighting difficult for both Union and Confederate soldiers.

LITTLE ROUND TOP

The battle at Little Round Top has become one of Gettysburg's most well-known events. The Union defended the hill. As Confederate troops advanced, the 20th Maine Regiment ran out of bullets. Out of options, they charged down the hill with only **bayonets.** This risky move pushed back the Confederates.

People report seeing ghostly soldiers on horseback at old battlefields around the world.

The ghosts of the men who died there may have never left. In 1995, a woman visited the site around 9:00 p.m. She gazed down the hill at Devil's Den. Suddenly, she felt someone behind her.

The woman slowly turned around. Behind her, a man sat on a horse. He wore a blue uniform and tall boots. His coat buttons glinted in the moonlight. She looked away for a moment. When she looked back again, the man had vanished. Had she seen a ghostly soldier?

GHOSTLY HELP?

The ghost of George Washington is said to have appeared to the 20th Maine Regiment. Washington was the first U.S. president. He died in 1799. As the soldiers marched toward Gettysburg, they came upon a fork in the road. They didn't know which road to take. Washington's ghost took them down the right path.

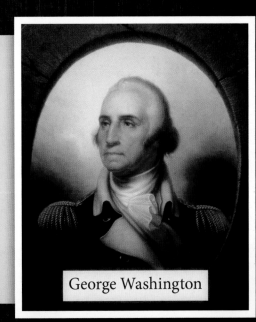

George Washington

CHAPTER 2
THE CASHTOWN INN

In late June 1863, Confederate soldiers gathered in Cashtown. The city was about 8 miles (13 kilometers) from Gettysburg. The soldiers needed rest. Confederate leaders checked into the Cashtown Inn.

On June 30, Confederate **scouts** returned to Cashtown from Gettysburg. The scouts reported that Union soldiers occupied the town. The Confederates decided to attack the Union. The next day, the Battle of Gettysburg began.

Wounded soldiers returned to Cashtown. Some were treated at the inn, which became a field hospital. Some say the ghosts of Confederate soldiers stayed behind.

The city of Cashtown was named after the Cashtown Inn. The inn's owner required cash payments.

Today, travelers can stay at the Cashtown Inn. But they might want to think twice about staying in Room 4. Many guests have reported ghostly activity in this room. A rapping sound at the door wakes guests in the night. When guests open the door, the hallway is empty. Some guests claim they've seen a ghostly Confederate soldier in the room. He's also been spotted in the hallway.

There may even be **evidence** that the inn is haunted. In the 1890s, a photograph was taken of the inn. A strange-looking man stands at the left side of the building. He wears what looks to be a Confederate uniform. Could it be the ghost of a soldier who fought at Gettysburg? Or could there be a reasonable explanation for the sighting, such as a **double exposure**?

Confederate soldiers typically wore a hat, a wool jacket, trousers, and leather shoes. They also carried their weapons and a small pack for personal items.

CHAPTER 3

GETTYSBURG COLLEGE

Gettysburg College sits in the heart of the city. During the Battle of Gettysburg, the campus became a field hospital. Some say the ghosts of the dead haunt the grounds. But it's not just home to Civil War spirits. The college also is said to attract other kinds of ghosts.

PENNSYLVANIA HALL

In the 1800s, students lived in the large building that is now called Pennsylvania Hall. During the battle, it became a field hospital. Doctors worked to save as many soldiers as they could. But many died there.

Pennsylvania Hall

In the late 1960s, Pennsylvania Hall became a campus office building. Late one night, two workers took the elevator to the first floor. But the elevator took them to the basement instead. The doors slowly opened to reveal a **grisly** scene.

As a field hospital, Gettysburg College hosted both Union and Confederate soldiers.

The basement was being used for storage. But it had changed into a Civil War hospital. Blood-stained men groaned on tables. Surgeons stitched them back up. The workers pushed the first-floor button, desperate to flee. Then a ghostly surgeon looked right at them. Finally, the doors slid closed. The elevator returned to the first floor. The terrified workers reported what they had seen. A guard went to the basement. There were no signs of any ghosts.

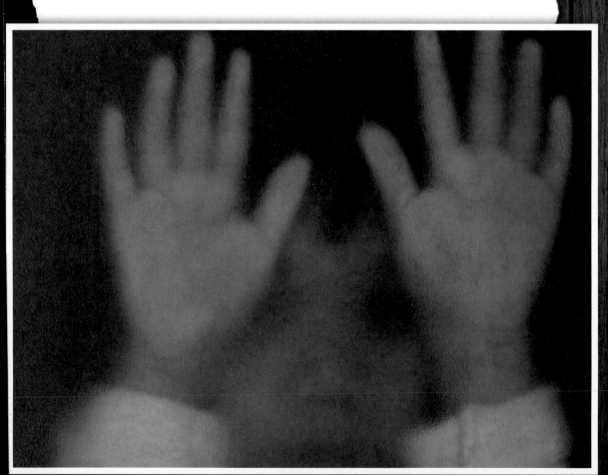

THE BLUE BOY

Stevens Hall at Gettysburg College opened in 1868 as a girls' school. Shortly after opening, some girls rescued a boy from a nearby orphanage. They hid him in their room on the third floor. One cold winter night, the **headmistress** of Stevens Hall knocked on their door. The girls had the boy crawl onto the window ledge to hide. The headmistress questioned the girls about the missing boy. After she left, the girls threw open the window. But the boy was gone. The snowy ground below held no footprints. The girls never saw the boy again.

Today, the hall is a dorm for the college. Many residents claim they've seen the boy's ghost. His bluish face hovers outside the third floor. He writes "help me" in the frost on the windows.

FREAKY FACT

Pennsylvania Hall has a rounded structure called a cupola on its roof. Confederate General Robert E. Lee may have used the cupola to view his troops. Students and staff have seen figures pacing on it at night. Did they see Confederate ghosts?

CHAPTER 4

GETTYSBURG NATIONAL CEMETERY

After the Battle of Gettysburg, dead soldiers were quickly buried in shallow graves. Local residents soon created a cemetery. More than 3,500 Union soldiers were buried there.

Union Captain William Miller is said to have haunted the cemetery for many years. Miller led the 3rd Pennsylvania **Cavalry**. He later won the Congressional Medal of Honor. After his death, Miller was buried at the cemetery. Park rangers and visitors have seen a dim figure that looked like Miller. In the 1970s, Miller's headstone was updated to include his award. After that, his ghost never appeared again. Perhaps the ghost received the recognition it was waiting for?

FREAKY FACT

On November 19, 1863, President Abraham Lincoln spoke at the cemetery. His speech became known as the Gettysburg Address.

Gettysburg National Cemetery was built on part of the battlefield.

WILLIAM E MILLER
MEDAL OF HONOR
CAPT CO H
3 PA CAV
DEC 10 1919

William Miller died of natural causes in 1919 at the age of 83.

Visitors say the dead still don't rest. One man visited at night. He heard a strange noise. Then he saw a blue ball of shimmering light. It floated about 4 feet (1.2 meters) off the ground. Suddenly, the light began moving toward him. The man ran all the way back to his hotel room.

CHAPTER 5

HAUNTED HOUSES

Haunting laughter. Strange noises. Ghostly figures. Some say Gettysburg is the most haunted town in America. Ghosts are said to haunt several houses in town.

THE JENNIE WADE HOUSE

On July 1, 1863, Jennie Wade fled her home on Breckenridge Street. She thought her house was too close to the fighting. She thought she'd be safer at her sister's house on Baltimore Street. On July 3, Union and Confederate lines closed in on the house. A stray bullet flew through the front door and kitchen door. The bullet struck Jennie while she was baking bread. She died instantly. Her family carried her body into the cellar. They hid there until the fighting ended.

Today, the Jennie Wade House is a popular tourist attraction in Gettysburg.

The house on Baltimore is now called the Jennie Wade House. Visitors to the historical home say her ghost lingers. People have witnessed a ghostly woman in the kitchen. They also smell freshly baked bread. Chains are moved by unseen hands. Doors close by themselves. In 2011, ghost hunters investigated the home's cellar. They filmed **orbs** floating along the ceiling. Many ghost hunters believe orbs are signs that ghosts are present. Had they seen Jennie's ghost?

People commonly report seeing ghosts in dark, dreary basements and cellars.

By 1869, there were more than 60 children at the Orphans' Homestead.

A HAUNTED ORPHANAGE

The Civil War ended on April 9, 1865. In 1866, the Orphans' Homestead opened in Gettysburg. It housed the children of Union soldiers killed in battle. Eleven years later, the orphanage was forced to close. Headmistress Rosa Carmichael treated the children poorly. She locked them in the dark basement if they misbehaved. Carmichael was later arrested for her crimes. Many people say ghosts haunt this house on Baltimore Street.

For years, the former orphanage operated as a museum. Today, it's owned by a ghost-hunting company. Many visitors and workers have reported ghostly activity. Children's laughter can be heard, even when no children are present. Ghostly children wearing Civil War-era clothing appear inside the house.

One visitor got quite the scare while touring the basement. He suddenly felt arms wrap around him from behind. But no one was there! Some believe it was the ghost of Rosa Carmichael, seeking revenge.

THE GHOSTS OF GETTYSBURG

Gettysburg was one of the bloodiest battles ever fought on U.S. soil. The battlefield and other places in the town of Gettysburg may be filled with the ghosts of those who died there. Or perhaps there are other explanations for the eerie happenings. Think about the stories, and decide for yourself!

HAUNTED WAX MUSEUM

Gettysburg once had a wax museum featuring U.S. presidents. Visitors claimed the museum was haunted. The figures of ghostly soldiers wandered the museum. The wax figures were said to move on their own. After the museum closed in 2016, the figures were sold.

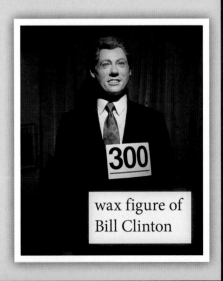

wax figure of Bill Clinton

Haunted Places of
GETTYSBURG

1. **Little Round Top**

2. **Devil's Den**

3. **National Cemetery**

4. **Jennie Wade House**

5. **Gettysburg College**

6. **Orphans' Homestead**

MORE HAUNTED PLACES

7. **Iverson's Pits**

   Iverson's Pits is a grassy field where many
   Confederates died. They were buried in
   shallow graves. Some say it's haunted.

8. **Spangler's Spring**

   Spangler's Spring was a natural spring on
   the battlefield. A woman in white is said
   to haunt it.

9. **Dobbin House Tavern**

   The Dobbin House Tavern is one of
   the oldest homes in Gettysburg. Three
   ghosts reportedly haunt the house.

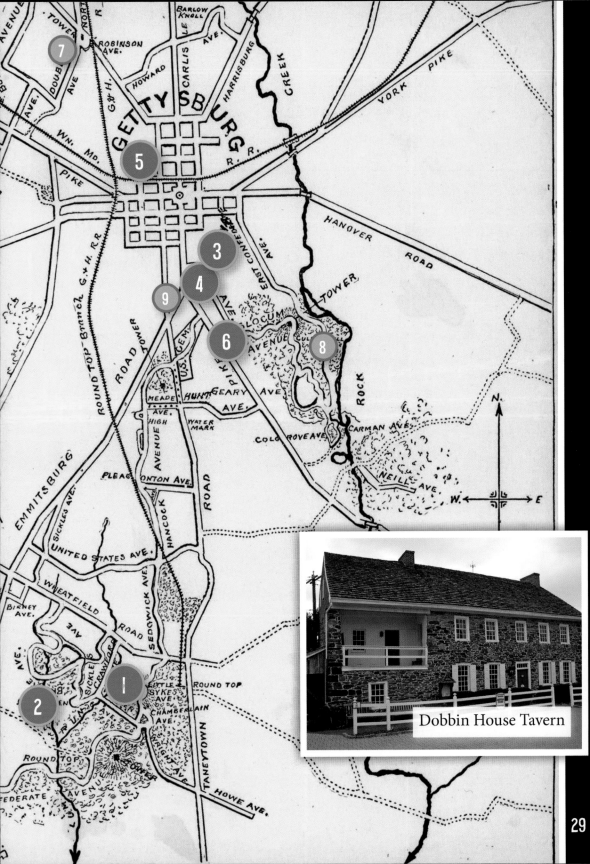

Dobbin House Tavern

GLOSSARY

bayonet (BAY-uh-net)—a long metal blade attached to the end of a musket or rifle

cavalry (KA-vuhl-ree)—a unit of soldiers who fight on horseback

civilian (si-VIL-yuhn)—a person who is not in the military

double exposure (DUH-bul ik-SPO-zhur)—a photography method in which two photographs are taken on the same piece of film

evidence (EV-uh-duhnss)—information, items, and facts that help prove something to be true or false

ghost (GOHST)—a spirit of a dead person believed to haunt people or places

grisly (GRIZ-lee)—something that inspires fear or disgust

headmistress (hed-MISS-truss)—a woman in charge of a private school

orb (AWRB)—a glowing ball of light that sometimes appears in photographs taken at reportedly haunted locations

regiment (REJ-uh-muhnt)—a large group of soldiers who fight together as a unit

scout (SKOWT)—a soldier who travels ahead of a military group to gather information about the enemy

trench (TRENCH)—a long, narrow ditch dug in the ground to serve as shelter from enemy fire or attack

READ MORE

Chandler, Matt. *Famous Ghost Stories of North America.* North Mankato, MN: Capstone Press, 2019.

Gagne, Tammy. *Ghosts of War.* North Mankato, MN: Capstone Press, 2018.

Summers, Alex. *Haunted Battlefields and Cemeteries.* Vero Beach, FL: Rourke Educational Media, 2016.

INTERNET SITES

National Geographic Kids: The Battle of Gettysburg.
https://kids.nationalgeographic.com/explore/history/gettysburg

National Park Service: Gettysburg.
https://www.nps.gov/gett/index.htm

Scary for Kids: Gettysburg.
https://www.scaryforkids.com/gettysburg

INDEX